C000193104

Introduction

Traditional Irish cookery brings to the minds of most people, Irish stew, boiled bacon and cabbage, and soda bread. Delightful and wholesome as these dishes may be, they do not fully portray the vast wealth of traditional cookery.

Years of poverty and hardship have stifled the innovativeness of the Irish cook. Old herbs and seasonings, such as sorrel and garlic, were lost to the Irish kitchen until recent years. Garlic grows wild in the west of Ireland, probably brought to Galway by the Spanish – along with their great love of the onion, a taste which hasn't been lost.

The idea, then, that all traditional cookery is simply frugal fare is a misbelief. There are also delicious 'noble' recipes which are no less a part of Irish heritage for being little known. In the following pages I have tried to include some unusual traditional dishes along with the good old faithfuls.

And, of course, if the Irishman isn't 'kitchen inclined', there is always an alternative open to him, the great pint of Irish stout! In the words of Flann O'Brien ...

When food is scarce
And your larder's bare,
And no rashers grease your pan,
When hunger grows
As your meals grow rare,
A pint of plain is your only man.

As they say, 'There's atin' and drinkin' in it.'

Notes on Ingredients

BACON: Either green or smoked bacon may be used in all recipes. The rind may be removed before cooking but was usually left on in traditional recipes.

BUTTERMILK: This is the liquid left from the cream from which butter has been made. If buttermilk is not available, sour milk may be substituted. To sour fresh milk, add half a teaspoon of lemon juice or vinegar to one pint of milk and leave in a warm place for ten to fifteen minutes. (Alternatively, see **Homemade Buttermilk** in **Miscellaneous** section.)

CARRAGEEN: Carrageen Moss (Chondrus Crispus) is a dark purplish seaweed. It grows on the rocks on the lower seashore — hence its name, *carraig* being the Irish for rock. In late spring it is gathered at low tide and bleached and dried in the sun. It has a high iodine and mineral content and is considered very beneficial to invalids.

CREAM: When cream is called for in a recipe, use either whipping cream or a half-and-half mix of single and double cream. Only one middle-fat content cream is available in Ireland.

DRIPPING: Where dripping is called for in a recipe, pork or beef dripping may be used. Mutton or lamb dripping may be used only in mutton or lamb dishes.

HERBS: When possible, it is always best to use fresh herbs. If dried herbs are used, halve the quantities given for fresh,

e.g. $\frac{1}{2}$ tsp. fresh $= \frac{1}{4}$ tsp. dried
$\frac{1}{4}$ tsp. fresh = pinch dried.

Quantities used are largely a matter of taste. Start by using a small amount and add more if taste so dictates. Wait at least 5 minutes between additions to allow flavours to infuse.

ROUND STEAK: Rump steak.

SCALLIONS: Spring onions.

STOCK: Beef, chicken or bacon (not salty) stocks were all interchanged, and basically whichever was available was used. If stock cubes are being used, chicken or vegetable is best for light dishes and beef for red meat dishes.

STOUT/PORTER: Dark brown beer made from roasted malt. Ireland's national drink (Guinness being the most famous brand).

WHISKEY MEASURES: An Irish measure of whiskey is $\frac{1}{4}$ gill, larger than its British counterpart, which is $\frac{1}{6}$ gill. So $1\frac{1}{2}$ British measures would be used in place of one Irish measure.

Measures and Conversions

IMPERIAL	METRIC
1 oz.	25 grammes (gm)
4 oz.	125 grammes
1 lb.	450 grammes
2¼ lbs.	1,000 grammes (1 kilo)
1 fl. oz.	25 ml.
1 pint (pt.), 20 fl. oz.	550 ml
1¾ pint	1 litre
1 teaspoon (tsp.)	5 ml.
1 dessertspoon (dsp.)	12 ml.
1 tablespoon (tbsp.)	15 ml.

Conversion equivalents are approximates – never use both metric and imperial measures in the same recipe.

OVEN TEMPERATURES

	Gas Mark	°C	°F
Cool	½	140/150	275/300
Moderate	4	180	350
Hot	7	220	425
Very hot	8/9	230/240	450/475

PORTIONS: All recipes cater for four, unless otherwise stated.

Soups

CREAM OF MUSSEL SOUP

$\frac{3}{4}$ pt. mussels
1$\frac{1}{2}$ pts. cold water
2 oz. butter
1 oz. flour
$\frac{1}{4}$ pt. single cream
salt and pepper

Wash the mussels thoroughly. Heat in a dry frying-pan until the shells open. Shell and beard mussels. In a saucepan melt butter, add flour and fry for 1 or 2 minutes. Remove from heat and stir in water, plus any liquid from frying pan. Add salt and pepper, bring to the boil, cover and simmer for 10 minutes. Remove from heat. Stir in mussels and cream. Adjust seasoning and serve immediately.

CHICKEN BROTH

1 boiling fowl
$\frac{1}{4}$ lb. split peas
$\frac{1}{4}$ lb. pearl barley
$\frac{1}{2}$ lb. onions
$\frac{1}{2}$ lb. carrots
1 small turnip
salt and pepper
$\frac{1}{4}$ lb. chopped, cooked bacon (optional)

Soak peas overnight. Wash fowl, place in pot with enough water to cover. Add the barley and rinsed, soaked peas. Cover and simmer for 3 to 4 hours. Skim if necessary. Peel and dice all vegetables, add to pot.

Bring back to the boil and simmer until fowl is tender. Remove fowl from pot. Skin and remove meat from bones. Return meat to broth and season to taste.

NETTLE SOUP

- 1 pt. nettle tops
- 1 oz. butter
- 1 oz. oatmeal
- 1 pt. water, stock or milk
- salt and pepper to taste

Wash the nettle tops in several changes of cold water. Chop finely or mince. Melt butter in pot. Sprinkle in oatmeal and fry until golden brown. Stir in water, stock or milk. Bring to the boil stirring continuously. Add the nettles, salt and pepper. Bring to the boil. Lower heat and simmer for 30 to 45 minutes.

ONION SOUP

- 2 lbs. onions
- 1 pt. water
- 1 pt. milk
- 1 oz. butter
- thick slice of bread
- salt and pepper

Slice onions and fry in butter until cooked but not browned. Add water, pepper, salt and bread. Bring to the boil, simmer for 20 minutes, rub through a sieve. Return to pot with milk. Heat to almost boiling and serve.

POTATO SOUP

$1\frac{1}{2}$ pts. water
1 pt. milk
$2\frac{1}{2}$ lbs. potatoes
1 lb. onions
pinch of thyme
1 whole clove
salt and pepper

Peel and slice potatoes and onions. Add to pot with water, thyme and the whole clove. Bring to the boil, cover and simmer for about an hour. Rub through a sieve. Stir in milk, salt and pepper. Heat through, without boiling, and serve.

TURNIP AND BACON SOUP

$\frac{1}{4}$ lb. streaky bacon – rinds removed
$\frac{1}{4}$ lb. chopped onions
$\frac{1}{4}$ lb. chopped potatoes
$\frac{3}{4}$ lb. chopped turnips
2 pts. stock
salt and pepper to taste
fat for frying

Chop and fry bacon and onions. Add potatoes, turnips and stock. Cook gently until vegetables are soft. Adjust seasoning and serve.

Fish

BAKED COD

    4 fillets of cod
    2 oz. butter
    4 large tomatoes
    1 tsp. chopped fresh thyme
    2 tbsps. water or fish stock
    salt and pepper

Place fillets in an ovenproof dish with water. Season and sprinkle with thyme. Slice tomatoes and place over fish. Dot with butter and cook in a moderate oven for 45 minutes to one hour.

BAKED SALMON

Ireland's legendary Finn MacCool is said to have 'gained the wisdom of the ages when he but licked a thumb that had burst a blister on the roasting "Salmon of Knowledge".' It is doubtful if this is the reason for the immense popularity of the 'King of Fish', but the Irish, who relish the eating of it, are certainly no fools.

    one 5-7 lb. salmon
    2 oz. butter
    juice of $\frac{1}{2}$ lemon
    2 tbsps. water
    salt and pepper

Season washed and gutted salmon with salt and pepper. Place in an ovenproof dish, add water and lemon juice and dot with butter. Cover with tinfoil. Bake for 1-1$\frac{1}{2}$ hours (12 minutes per lb.) at 400°F,

200°C or Gas Mark 6. Remove skin and serve either hot or cold.

BUTTERED KIPPERS

4 kippers
water to cover
butter

Place kippers in pan. Pour in enough boiling water to cover, and simmer gently for 1 or 2 minutes. Serve with knobs of melting butter and plenty of fresh soda bread.

CREAMED PLAICE

4 large or 8 small fillets of plaice
2 oz. butter
$\frac{1}{4}$ pt. sour cream
2 tbsp. milk
1 tbsp. chopped chives
salt and pepper

Season fish, using plenty of pepper. Place in an ovenproof dish and add milk and butter cut up into small pieces. Bake for 30-40 minutes in a low oven. Add cream and chopped chives and serve immediately.

FRIED TROUT

4 rainbow trout
seasoned flour
butter for frying

Wash and pat dry trout. Roll in seasoned flour and fry in butter for about five minutes on each side. Serve with mashed potatoes into which two tablespoons of chives have been mixed.

GARLIC MACKEREL

  4 large or 8 small filleted mackerel
  1 clove garlic
  seasoned flour
  a little beaten egg
  butter for frying
  lemon juice

Mince garlic very finely. Divide between the fish and rub in well. Roll mackerel in beaten egg and then in flour. Fry in butter for 4-5 minutes each side. Sprinkle with lemon juice and serve.

HERRINGS IN OATFLAKES

  4 filleted herrings
  4 oz. oatmeal flakes – seasoned
  lemon juice
  butter for frying

Roll herrings in oatflakes, fry in hot butter for 3-4 minutes each side and serve sprinkled with lemon juice. Alternatively, bake for 20 minutes in a moderate oven, dotted with butter. Mackerel is also delicious cooked in this way.

HOT BUTTERED MUSSELS

  2 pts. mussels
  3-4 oz. butter
  salt and pepper
  2 tbsps. chopped chives

Wash mussels thoroughly under running water. Remove 'beards' and discard any open shells. Place mussels in pan and cook over a high temperature for 7 or 8 minutes until the shells open. Season with salt and pepper. Place in a serving dish and pour cooking juices over. Dot with knobs of butter and sprinkle with chopped chives. Serve with fresh brown bread and butter.

SMOKED COD PIE
1 lb. smoked cod
$\frac{1}{2}$ lb. onions
$\frac{1}{2}$ lb. shelled peas
$\frac{1}{2}$ pt. milk or $\frac{1}{4}$ pt. milk and $\frac{1}{4}$ pt. single cream
1 oz. flour
1 tsp. mustard powder
1 oz. butter
2 lbs. mashed potato

Chop onions roughly and fry in butter until tender. Remove from heat and stir in flour and mustard. Add milk. Return to heat and stir until thickened. Add cod, cut into 1-2 inch cubes, and peas. Turn into ovenproof dish and cover with mashed potatoes. Bake in a moderate oven at 400°F, 200°C, Gas Mark 6, for 30-45 minutes until golden brown.

Although not traditional, the addition of 2-3 oz. of Cheddar cheese to the sauce makes this an extremely tasty dish.

STEAMED OYSTERS
2 oz. oysters
$\frac{1}{4}$ pt. boiling water
2 oz. melted butter

Scrub oyster shells to remove all sand. Spread out on a

large, shallow pan. Pour over boiling water. Cover and simmer over low heat until shells are open. Serve with a dish of melted butter, brown bread and butter.

STUFFED TROUT

    4 rainbow trout
    4 oz. breadcrumbs
    2 oz. chopped onion
    1 tbsp chopped parsley
    $\frac{1}{4}$ tsp. grated lemon rind
    juice of $\frac{1}{2}$ lemon
    1 egg yolk
    salt and pepper
    a little butter

Fry onion gently in butter until transparent. Mix with all stuffing ingredients. Season trout and fill with stuffing mixture. Place in an ovenproof dish and bake for 1 hour at 400°F, 200°C or Gas Mark 6. Serve with cooking juices poured over and a sprinkling of parsley.

Pork and Bacon

BLACK PUDDING

Always served with an Irish 'fry'. The preparation of this pudding may be impractical these days due to the difficulty of procuring fresh pigs' blood and casings.

1 lb. pigs' liver
1½ lbs. unrendered lard, chopped
6 pts. pigs' blood
2 lbs. breadcrumbs
4 oz. oatmeal
4 oz. wheatenmeal
1 medium onion, chopped
1 tsp. salt
½ tsp. allspice
beef casings

Stew liver in boiling salted water until tender. Remove liver and mince. Reserve cooking liquor. Mix all ingredients in large bowl. Stir thoroughly until blended. Fill casings with mixture. Tie off in one-foot loops. Steam for 4-5 hours. Leave until cold. Cut into ½ inch slices as required and fry in hot fat on both sides until crisped.

BOILED BACON AND CABBAGE

By far the most popular traditional dish, and there is nothing to beat this simple, satisfying meal on a cold winter's day.

2-3 lbs. collar of bacon
1 medium-sized cabbage

Soak bacon overnight in cold water. Place in a pot, cover with fresh water and bring to the boil. Remove scum. Cover and simmer for 1½ hours (30 minutes per lb.). Cut cabbage into quarters and add to pot. Cook gently for about ½ hour or until cabbage is cooked to your liking. Drain and serve with potatoes boiled in their jackets.

A couple of cloves may be added to the bacon along with the cabbage, but remove them before serving.

CODDLE
The true Dubliner's Saturday Supper

$\frac{1}{4}$ lb. streaky bacon rashers
$\frac{1}{4}$ lb. pork sausages (left whole)
$\frac{3}{4}$ lb. onions
2 lbs. small potatoes
1 pt. water
salt and pepper
fat for frying

Fry chopped bacon, sausages and coarsely chopped onions in the fat until the onions are golden. Peel small potatoes and add to the onions. Pour on the water. Season, cover, simmer until potatoes are cooked.

CRUIBÍNS – pronounced
CRUBEENS (PIGS' TROTTERS)
These were traditionally eaten in pubs on a Saturday evening, but unfortunately this custom has died out.

8 pigs' trotters
3-4 tsps. salt

Wash trotters thoroughly. Cover with water and soak overnight. Rinse and cover with fresh cold water in a large pot. Bring to the boil. Remove scum. Lower heat and simmer for 2-3 hours or until tender. Drain and serve hot with freshly prepared mustard and bread and butter.

DUBLIN STEWED PORK

1½ lbs. pork pieces or pork skirts (skin removed)
2 lbs. cooking apples
1 lb. onions
1 tbsp. brown sugar
¼ pt. stock or water
¼ pt. cream
seasoned flour
butter or bacon fat for frying

Chop meat and onion into rough pieces. Melt the fat or butter and gently fry onion until tender. Remove from pan. Toss the meat in seasoned flour and brown quickly in hot fat. Place onions, meat, stock and sugar in a pot and simmer, covered for 1½ hours. Peel, core and chop apples. Add to pot. Continue cooking until apples are just cooked but not too mushy. Add cream and heat through. Do not boil. Correct seasoning and serve.

GAMMON STEAKS WITH WHISKEY SAUCE

4 gammon steaks
2 tbsps. very finely chopped onion
1 tbsp. brown sugar
1 tbsp. whiskey
1 oz. flour
1 oz. butter
¼ pt. water or stock
salt and pepper to taste

Brush steaks with melted butter. Snip fat to prevent curling and grill for 7-8 minutes each side.

To make sauce, gently fry onions in remainder of

16

butter until cooked. Remove from heat and stir in flour gradually. Add stock. Return to heat. Add sugar and bring to the boil. Simmer gently for about 2 minutes to cook flour. If sauce seems a little thick, add more water. Add whiskey and season to taste. Place gammon steaks on a warmed serving dish and pour on sauce.

Serve with peas and carrots and sauté potatoes.

KERRY CASSEROLE

$\frac{3}{4}$ lb. belly of pork
$\frac{3}{4}$ lb. smoked bacon
2 lbs. potatoes
1 lb. onions
$\frac{1}{4}$ lb. mushrooms
$\frac{1}{4}$ pt. stock
1 tsp. fresh rosemary
salt and pepper
2 oz. butter

Cut meat into one-inch cubes. Peel and thinly slice potatoes. Finely chop onions. Peel or wipe mushrooms and slice if large. Grease an ovenproof dish with some of the butter and place a layer of sliced potatoes in the bottom. Add half the meat pieces, seasoned and sprinkled with rosemary. Layer with half the vegetables, plus another layer of potatoes. Repeat, using all meat, vegetables and potatoes. Pour stock over and dot potatoes with remaining butter.

Cover and cook in a moderate oven, 325°F, 160°C or Gas Mark 3 for $2\frac{1}{2}$ hours. Uncover for last $\frac{1}{2}$ hour of cooking to brown potatoes.

LIVER AND BACON

$\frac{1}{2}$ lb. liver
$\frac{1}{2}$ lb. bacon rashers
1 lb. onions
$\frac{1}{2}$ pt. water or stock
seasoned flour
pinch of thyme
fat for frying

Wash and dry liver. Cut into thin slices and roll in seasoned flour. Cut onions into thin rings and bacon into one-inch pieces. Sauté onions in fat until tender. Layer ingredients in an ovenproof dish and pour on stock or water. Bake, covered, in a moderate oven for about 2 hours. Serve with mashed potatoes.

SPARE RIBS

$2\frac{1}{2}$ lbs. spare ribs
2 tsps. brown sugar
$\frac{1}{2}$ tsp. ground cloves
1 tsp. mustard powder

Place ribs in a large pot. Cover with cold water. Bring to the boil. Remove any scum from water. Cover and simmer for $1\frac{1}{2}$-2 hours or until meat is tender. Mix brown sugar, ground cloves and mustard powder. Drain ribs, place in an ovenproof dish and sprinkle lightly with spiced sugar. Brown in a very hot oven for 10-15 mins.

Lamb

CREAMED LAMB WITH MINT AND PEAS

$1\frac{1}{2}$ lbs. boned shoulder of lamb, sliced
$\frac{1}{4}$ pt. milk
$\frac{1}{4}$ pt. single cream
1 lb. shelled peas
6 young mint tops
2 oz. seasoned flour
salt and pepper
1 oz. dripping

Heat dripping in a pan. Roll lamb, sliced, in seasoned flour. Cook very gently for 15 minutes, stirring to prevent flour burning. In a large pot cook peas and mint in just enough, lightly salted boiling water to cover for 5 minutes. Strain. Add milk and bring to just under boiling point. Remove lamb from pan and strain off as much fat as possible. Add to peas and milk. Stir gently for 2-3 minutes. Stir in cream, season, heat through and serve.

IRISH STEW

1 lb. lean mutton pieces
1 lb. onions
1 lb. carrots
1 lb. potatoes
salt and pepper
pinch of thyme

Place mutton with thyme in saucepan and add cold water to cover. Bring slowly to the boil and simmer for one hour. Add onions, potatoes, carrots, all peeled and roughly chopped. Season. Continue cooking until vegetables are tender. Adjust seasoning. May be served alone or with green cabbage or sprouts.

LAMBS' KIDNEYS IN PORT

    4 lambs' kidneys
    $\frac{1}{2}$ lb. mushrooms
    $\frac{1}{4}$ lb. finely chopped onion
    2 tbsps. port
    4 tbsps. water
    2 oz. butter
    $\frac{1}{2}$ oz. flour
    salt and pepper

Skin and core the kidneys, slice thinly. Wipe and slice mushrooms. Melt the butter in a pan and fry the onions until soft. Add the kidneys and mushrooms and fry for 2-3 minutes. Stir in the flour, add water, stirring constantly, and lastly add the port. Heat through. Season and serve with toast.

    Believe it or not, this was a breakfast dish for the gentry!

MUTTON CHOPS WITH BUTTER BEANS

    $\frac{1}{2}$ lb. butter beans
    $\frac{1}{4}$ lb. onions, finely chopped
    2 oz. butter
    4 large gigot chops
    $\frac{1}{2}$ tsp. chopped rosemary
    4 large tomatoes
    $\frac{1}{4}$ pt. water or stock
    1 oz. dripping
    salt and pepper

Prepare and cook butter beans as in recipe under **Vegetables**. Brown the chops in the dripping. Place half the beans in the bottom of an ovenproof dish, followed by the chops. Sprinkle with rosemary, salt and pepper. Thickly slice tomatoes and lay over chops. Cover with remaining beans. Pour stock or water over, tightly cover and cook for $1\frac{1}{2}$ hours in a moderate oven.

PICKLED LAMBS' TONGUE

    8 lambs' tongues
    4 tbsps. salt
    pinch of saltpetre
    2 pts. cold water
    4-6 whole cloves
    8 peppercorns
    1 bay leaf
    1 sprig of rosemary

Dissolve the salt in the water. Add the saltpetre and the lambs' tongues. After two days remove tongues. Cover with cold water. Add the cloves, peppercorns, bay leaf and rosemary. Bring to the boil, cover and simmer for one hour. Drain. Discard herbs and spices.

    Serve hot with onion sauce.

ROAST LEG OF LAMB WITH MUSTARD

    1-3 lb. leg of lamb
    1 tsp. mustard powder
    1 tbsp. seasoned flour
    2 oz. dripping

Pre-heat the oven to 180°C, 350°F, Gas Mark 4. Put the dripping into the roasting tin and place in oven. Mix the mustard powder with the flour. Wipe meat and rub all over with the mustard/flour mix. Quickly remove tin from oven and roll joint in the hot fat to sear. Place meat in the tin and return to the oven for $1\frac{1}{2}$-$1\frac{3}{4}$ hours, basting every $\frac{1}{2}$ hour.

Beef

BEEF STEW WITH DUMPLINGS

$1\frac{1}{2}$ lbs. stewing or rib steak
2 lbs. onions
1 lb. carrots
1 tsp. vinegar
1 tsp. brown sugar
1 tsp. chopped sage
1 clove garlic
$\frac{1}{2}$ tsp. mustard
1 pt. rich brown stock
Seasoned flour

Dumplings
12 oz. flour
$\frac{1}{2}$ tsp. salt
$\frac{1}{2}$ tsp. bicarbonate of soda
4 oz. suet

Trim meat and cut into one-inch cubes. Peel and roughly chop onions and carrots. Heat dripping in pan. Roll beef in seasoned flour and quickly brown all over in the dripping. Remove from pan and place in a saucepan. Brown onion and add to saucepan, also with stock and all other ingredients, except carrots. Cook gently for $1\frac{1}{2}$ hours. Add the carrots. Now mix together the dumpling ingredients, adding enough water to make a soft dough. Add balls of dough, about the size of a tablespoon, to the stew. Simmer uncovered for 10 minutes. Cover the pot and simmer for a further 15 minutes.

MINCED BEEF AND ONION PIE

    1 lb. minced beef
    ½ lb. onion
    pinch each of parsley, sage, thyme
    ¼ pt. stout
    1 oz. flour
    1 oz. dripping
    sage and pepper
    12 oz. shortcrust pastry
    egg for glazing

Chop onion and fry in dripping. Add mince and brown for 2 or 3 minutes. Sprinkle in herbs. Stir in flour and add stout. Season well and cook gently for 30 minutes. Pre-heat oven to 400°F, 200°C, Gas Mark 6. Line a 9-inch pie tin with slightly over half the shortcrust pastry, fill with minced meat and cover with the rest of the pastry, fork edges. Glaze pie with lightly beaten egg and cut a small cross in the centre. Pastry scraps may be used to decorate the pie. Bake for 30-40 minutes.

PORTER BEEF

The addition of porter or stout to this stew gives it a really rich flavour – no wonder it was a very popular Saturday-night dish for Dubliners arriving home from the market stalls after a day's selling in typically Irish weather! It would be cooked beforehand and re-heated – worth trying, as the flavour is definitely enhanced by doing so.

2 lbs. rib steak
1½ lbs. onions
½ lb. mushrooms
seasoned flour
½ pt. porter
½ pt. stock or water
1 tsp. brown sugar
pinch of nutmeg
salt and pepper
fat for frying

Cut meat into fairly large chunks and roll in seasoned flour. Brown in hot fat and remove from pot. Chop onions roughly and fry gently for 2-3 minutes. Return meat to pot. Add all other ingredients. Bring to the boil, reduce heat and simmer gently for 2 hours or until meat is tender.

POT ROAST OF BRISKET

Traditionally, this pot roast was cooked in a bastaple – a heavy iron pot with a lid which hung over the fire from an adjustable chain. A heavy pot with tightfitting lid will suffice these days

2 lbs. boned, rolled brisket
1 lb. onions
½ lb. carrots
½ lb. broad beans
½ pt. stock

pinch of thyme
$\frac{1}{2}$ tsp. mustard powder
seasoned flour
1 tbsp. dripping,
salt and pepper

Mix the thyme, mustard and seasoned flour and roll joint in the mix. Fry meat quickly on all sides in hot dripping. Remove from the pot. Brown quartered onions and carrots in pot for 2-3 minutes. Season and place meat on top and pour on stock. Bring to boil, then reduce heat. Cover tightly and cook very gently for 2-2$\frac{1}{2}$ hours. Check pot from time to time and add more water if necessary to stop burning. Half an hour before the meat is cooked, add broad beans. Serve with baked jacket potatoes.

PRESSED TONGUE

1 pickled ox tongue
1 medium onion
1 carrot
4 cloves
1 tbsp. sugar
a few peppercorns

Place tongue in a saucepan, cover with cold water and bring to the boil. Discard the water and cover again with fresh water. Alternatively, soak overnight in cold water. Bring to the boil, and add all other ingredients. Cover and simmer for about 3 hours. When cooked, plunge tongue into cold water (this makes it easier to remove the skin). Remove the skin and any gristle and bones. Place in a round cake tin. Cover with a plate and place a weight on top. Slice when cold and serve with hot mustard. If the tongue is not pickled, omit first boiling — just wash it thoroughly and cook for 4-4$\frac{1}{2}$ hours.

SPICED BEEF

A Christmas dish. This beef was prepared in a large joint to last over the festive season. It needs to be started two to three weeks in advance and is now normally bought ready-prepared from a butcher.

    10-14 lbs. corned silverside of beef
    $\frac{1}{2}$ oz. saltpetre
    1 lb. salt
    $\frac{1}{2}$ lb. demerara sugar
    $\frac{1}{4}$ lb. ground allspice

Rub sugar well into beef and leave for 12 hours. Rub in salt. Leave for 12 hours. Baste well. Continue to baste well every day for 2 to 3 weeks. Weigh beef and place in a large pot. Cover with cold water and bring to the boil. Cover pot and simmer, allowing 30 minutes per lb. plus 30 minutes. May be eaten hot or cold. If the pot is too small for the beef, cut the joint into smaller pieces and cook individually.

STEAK AND MUSHROOM PIE

    $\frac{1}{2}$ lb. mushrooms, sliced
    1$\frac{1}{2}$ lbs. minced steak
    $\frac{1}{4}$ lb. bacon
    1 lb. onions, finely chopped
    1 oz. flour
    1$\frac{1}{2}$ lbs. mashed potatoes

salt and pepper
$\frac{1}{2}$ tsp. each parsley,
    sage, thyme
$\frac{1}{4}$ tsp. rosemary
2 tbsps. strong stock
1 oz. dripping

} use half quantities of herbs if dried

Heat dripping in pot. Add onions and fry until soft. Add meat and bacon. Mix in the herbs and cook for $\frac{1}{2}$ hour. Mix flour with stock until very smooth, and stir into mince. Season. Remove from heat. Add mushrooms and place the mix in a large ovenproof dish. Spoon on mashed potatoes. Even off the top with a fork. Dot with butter and cook in a moderate oven for 45 minutes to an hour. Serve with green peas.

STEWED STEAK AND ONIONS
$1\frac{1}{2}$-2 lbs. rib steak
1 lb. onions
$\frac{1}{2}$ tsp. sugar
salt and pepper
$\frac{1}{2}$ pt. stock
2 oz. dripping
1 oz. flour

Slice onions into rings and fry in dripping until brown. Remove from pan. Quickly brown steak on both sides. Sprinkle on flour and add stock and seasonings. Return onions to the pan and simmer for 2-2$\frac{1}{2}$ hours or until meat is very tender. Serve with peas and mashed potatoes.

STUFFED ROUND STEAK

2 lbs. round steak (one piece)
2 cups of breadcrumbs
$\frac{1}{2}$ lb. finely chopped onion
1 tsp. chopped parsley
1 tsp. chopped thyme
$\frac{1}{4}$ lb. finely chopped mushrooms
salt and pepper
1 pt. stock

Trim steak and flatten with a rolling pin. When quite thin, fill with stuffing, made by mixing all the other ingredients, except stock. Fold over and secure with skewers. Sear steak on all sides in hot fat. Place in an ovenproof dish, add stock and cook for 2-2$\frac{1}{2}$ hours in a moderate oven 325°F, 160°C, Mark 3.

TRIMLESTOWN ROAST SIRLOIN

A truly rich and delicious dish. This was to be seen only on the nobleman's table!

3 lbs. sirloin roast
2 fluid oz. whiskey
$\frac{1}{4}$ pt. red wine
1 oz. butter
2 oz. flour
salt and pepper

Preheat oven to 180°C, 350°F, Gas Mark 4. Wipe meat, season and place in a roasting tin. Place tin in oven and cook for one hour. Add the whiskey and wine to the pan. Cook for a further hour, basting once more. Remove the roast from the tin, place on a serving dish and keep warm. Pour off excess fat from the meat juices, adding water to bring to about $\frac{3}{4}$ pint. Beat the butter into the flour to form a smooth paste. Add a little of the juices to this and mix well, then pour onto juices, mixing again and bring to the boil. Simmer gently for 2-3 minutes to cook flour. Correct seasoning. If the sauce seems a little thick for your liking, add some more water. Serve separately in a gravy boat. Jacket or mashed potatoes and a plain cooked green vegetable, such as peas or broccoli, go best with this dish, as the sauce is so very rich.

Poultry and Game

BREAKFAST DUCK

In northern areas of the country this was the traditional Christmas morning breakfast.

    1 duck
    4 rashers of streaky bacon
    1 small onion, studded
    with 6 cloves
    2 tbsps. water
    salt and pepper

Pre-heat oven to 200°C, 400°F, Gas Mark 6. Wash and dry duck, season. Place the onion inside the duck. Truss and place in a roasting tin with the water. Lay the bacon over the duck, cover and roast for 45 minutes. Uncover, baste and roast open for a further 30-45 minutes at 180°C, 350°F, Gas Mark 4. Serve with unbuttered soda bread.

CASSEROLED CHICKEN WITH POTATO STUFFING

1-3 lbs. chicken

Stuffing:

1 lb. cooked potatoes
$\frac{1}{2}$ lb. chopped onion
$\frac{1}{4}$ lb. chopped bacon
$\frac{1}{4}$ lb. mushrooms, sliced
$\frac{1}{2}$ tsp. parsley
$\frac{1}{2}$ tsp. sage
1 egg
2 oz. butter
$\frac{1}{4}$ pt. stock
salt and pepper

Make stuffing by lightly frying onions, mushrooms and bacon in the butter. Add seasoning. Mash into the potatoes, pouring in all the butter from the pan. Season. Wash and dry chicken. Stuff and truss. Place in a casserole dish with $\frac{1}{4}$ pint of stock. Cover and place in a pre-heated oven 160°C, 325°F, Gas Mark 3, for 2 hours. Serve with braised celery and garden peas.

CHICKEN AND VEGETABLE PIE

$\frac{3}{4}$ lb. cooked chicken meat
$\frac{1}{4}$ streaky bacon rashers, chopped
1 lb. onions, chopped
$\frac{1}{2}$ lb. peas
$\frac{1}{2}$ lb. carrots
2 oz. butter
1 tsp. chopped parsley

1 oz. flour
½ pt. milk
1½ lbs. mashed potato
salt and pepper

Cook peas and thinly sliced carrots in salted, boiling water for 10 minutes. Strain. Fry onion and bacon in 1 oz. butter until cooked. Stir in flour slowly. Add milk and bring to boil. Remove from heat. Stir in chicken meat, parsley and vegetables. Place in an ovenproof dish. Cover with potato and even off with a fork. Dot with remaining butter. Heat through in a moderate to hot oven until golden.

RABBIT WITH MUSTARD SAUCE

4 rabbit joints
¼ pt. white wine
2 tsps. mustard powder
¼ pt. strong chicken stock
4 large tomatoes
½ tsp. sugar
2 large onions, quartered
¼ pt. cream
salt and pepper
2 oz. butter
chopped parsley

Roll rabbit joints in seasoned flour and brown in heated butter. Remove from pan and place in a casserole dish. Stir any remaining flour and the mustard into butter in pan and slowly add the stock and wine. Bring to the boil and remove from heat. Peel tomatoes by plunging them into boiling water for one minute. Chop very finely and add to sauce. Stir in parsley and $\frac{1}{2}$ teaspoon of sugar. Place the quartered onions around the rabbit in casserole and pour sauce over. Cover and cook in a moderate oven for $1\frac{1}{2}$ hours. Just before serving, check seasoning and stir cream into sauce. Sprinkle with chopped parsley.

ROAST STUFFED CHICKEN
    1-3 lbs. chicken
    1 oz. dripping
    1 oz. seasoned flour
Stuffing:
    1 large onion
    2 cups breadcrumbs
    $\frac{1}{2}$ tsp. each sage, thyme, parsley
    pinch of nutmeg
    salt and pepper
    3 oz. butter
Pre-heat oven to 220°C, 425°F, Gas Mark 7. Fry onion in butter until soft. Add herbs and seasonings. Mix with breadcrumbs and use to stuff the washed and dried chicken. Season skin of chicken and place in a roasting tin; cook for $\frac{1}{2}$ hour and then reduce oven temperature to 180°C, 350°F, Mark 4, and cook for a further 45 minutes, basting 2 or 3 times. 15 minutes before the bird is cooked, lightly rub the skin with seasoned flour and baste.

ROAST VENISON

1 haunch or shoulder of venison
4 oz. butter
flour and water
greaseproof paper

Marinade:

$\frac{1}{2}$ lb. onions
$\frac{1}{2}$ lb. carrots
2 tsps. chopped parsley
2 cloves garlic
2 tsps. thyme
1 bay leaf
8 black peppercorns
8 coriander seeds
4 juniper berries
juice and rind of 1 lemon
1 pt. red wine
$\frac{1}{4}$ pt. vegetable oil
2 tsps. brown sugar

Roughly chop vegetables. Crush garlic and chop herbs. Grate rind from lemon and squeeze lemon for juice. Mix together with all other marinade ingredients. Remove fat from joint. Place venison in a crock and cover with marinade. Turn in marinade 3-4 times a day. For mild flavour, marinate for 24 hours; for a stronger, more gamey flavour, marinate for 48 hours.

After desired marinating time, remove venison and wipe dry. Spread joint all over with softened butter. Wrap in greaseproof paper. Cover this greaseproof with a thick flour-and-water paste. Cover with another sheet — or sheets — of greaseproof and tie securely with string. Roast on a rack in a moderate oven 180°C, 350°F, Gas Mark 4 for 20 minutes per pound. This will give a medium-rare roast at which venison is tender. 20 minutes before the end of cooking time, remove joint from oven and discard greaseproof and paste layers. Dredge lightly with flour and return to oven to finish cooking. Serve with roast potatoes, gravy (made from thickening some of the marinade) and redcurrant or cranberry jelly. Serve very hot as venison fat is unpleasant when cool.

STUFFED RABBIT – ARMAGH STYLE
    1 rabbit
    2 oz. butter
    1-2 oz. flour
    $\frac{1}{2}$ pt. stock
Stuffing:
    2 cups breadcrumbs
    1 large onion
    2 large cooking apples
    2 tsps. parsley
    1 tsp. thyme
    1 tbsp. sugar
    1 tsp. salt
    1 oz. butter
    1 egg
    pepper to taste

Wash and dry rabbit. Chop onions and fry gently in 2 oz. of the butter. Peel apples and chop into onions. Fry until soft. Mix onion, apple and butter with all other stuffing ingredients, and brown quickly in remaining butter. Place in a casserole dish with well-seasoned stock and cook for 1¾ hours, or until tender, at 350°F, 180°C, Gas Mark 4.

TYRONE ROAST GOOSE

   1 goose
   6 cups breadcrumbs
   3 tsps. sage
   ½ lb. chopped cooked bacon
   4 oz. butter
   4 finely chopped shallots
   2 eggs
   salt and pepper
   ½ lemon

Wash and dry goose. Cut off any excess fat from around neck cavity. Prick skin all over. Rub skin with lemon and season. Fry shallots in butter until softened; mix with breadcrumbs, sage and bacon, season and bind with eggs and use to stuff bird. Sew up. Place in a very hot oven, 240°C, 475°F, Gas Mark 9, for 10 minutes. Reduce heat to 170°C, 340°F, Gas Mark 3 and cook for 3½-4 hours. Serve with apple sauce.

Potatoes

Nowhere in Irish cookery is there found such versatility as in the treatment of the humble potato. The potato, spud, pratie or Murphy can be served in some form or other at every meal.

The Irish like their potatoes floury, and Golden Wonders and Kerr's Pinks fit the bill admirably.

In the old peasant kitchen the main meal of the day would very often be a large pot of 'Smiling Murphies' (potatoes so floury that they had burst their jackets whilst cooking) and large mugs of buttermilk. The potatoes were cooked over the turf fire in a pot called a bastaple. They were then drained and emptied straight onto the table! Nowadays you are still unlikely to be served up a meal without its being accompanied by the faithful old spud, albeit presented in a daintier fashion.

APPLE MASH
  1 lb. cooking apples
  2 lbs. potatoes
  1 tbsp. sugar
  2 oz. butter

Peel potatoes. Cook in salted, boiling water. Meanwhile, peel, core and slice apples. Place in a pot with a tablespoon of water and the sugar. Cook until soft. When the potatoes are cooked, drain and mash thoroughly. Beat in the apples and butter. This mash goes particularly well with bacon or fried herrings.

BOXTY
  Boxty on the griddle,
  Boxty on the pan,
  If you don't eat boxty
  You'll never get a man!

  an old Irish saying.

½ lb. raw potato
½ lb. mashed potato
½ lb. plain flour
a little milk
1 egg
salt and pepper

Grate raw potatoes and mix with the cooked mashed potatoes. Add salt, pepper and flour. Beat eggs and add to mixture with enough milk to make a dropping batter. Drop by tablespoonfuls onto a hot griddle or frying pan. Cook over a moderate heat for 3-4 minutes on each side.

CHAMP OR POUNDIES

4 lbs. potatoes
½ lb. chopped scallions (spring onions)
½ pt. milk
2 tsps. salt
4 oz. butter
pepper

Champ is served piled high on the dish with a well of butter in the centre. It is eaten with a spoon from the outside, each spoonful being dipped in the well of melted butter.

Peel potatoes and cook in boiling water. Simmer milk and scallions for 5 minutes. Strain potatoes and mash thoroughly. Add hot milk and scallions, salt, pepper and half the butter.

The traditional implement used for pounding potatoes was a wooden masher known as a beetle.

COLCANNON (CALLY)

Did you ever eat Colcannon
When 'twas made from thickened cream,
And the kale and praties blended
Like the picture in a dream?
Did you ever take a forkful
And dip it in the lake
Of the clover-flavoured butter
That your mother used to make?

4 lbs. potatoes
1 lb. cooked curly kale, or savoy cabbage
1 oz. butter
½ pt. milk
6 chopped scallions (spring onions)

Peel and boil potatoes. Drain and mash until smooth. Add scallions to milk and bring to boil. Add to potato and beat well until fluffy. Beat in finely chopped kale and butter. Re-heat if necessary. Serve with butter.

FLUFFY MASHED POTATOES

2 lbs. potatoes
¼ pt. milk
2 oz. butter
salt and pepper

Peel potatoes. Bring to the boil in salted water and simmer until cooked. Drain well and mash. Bring the milk to the boil, add to the mashed potatoes and beat until fluffy. Season and serve with the butter melting on top.

POTATO CAKES (SLIM)

    1 lb. potatoes
    2 tsps. salt
    1 oz. butter
    4 oz. flour (approx.)
    1 egg

Boil the potatoes. Drain and mash to remove all lumps. Add the salt and butter, and work in as much flour as the potatoes will absorb. This will vary according to moistness of potatoes. Turn onto a floured surface and knead lightly. Roll into rounds $\frac{1}{4}$ inch thick and cook on a griddle or heavy-based frying pan until lightly browned on each side — about 10-15 minutes. Serve immediately thickly buttered or alternatively fry cold 'Slim' in hot bacon fat until golden.

Vegetables

BABY CARROTS AND ONIONS IN CREAM

    1 lb. baby carrots
    1 lb. small white onions
    $\frac{1}{4}$ pt. cream
    salt and pepper
    $\frac{1}{2}$ tsp. sugar
    pinch of nutmeg

Wash and trim carrots. Peel onions. Place in pot with $\frac{1}{2}$ inch boiling salted water. Cover and simmer gently for 10 minutes. Remove lid and boil rapidly, shaking pot to prevent burning, until water is absorbed. Stir in

cream and add pepper and salt to taste, if necessary.
Serve with a very light sprinkling of nutmeg.

BAKED PARNIPS
    $2\frac{1}{2}$ lbs. parsnips
    2 oz. butter or bacon fat
    3 tbsps. stock
    salt and pepper
    pinch of nutmeg

Peel parsnips, quarter and remove any woody core.
Parboil for 15 minutes. Place in an ovenproof dish.
Add stock and sprinkle with salt, pepper and nutmeg.
Dot with butter and bake for 30 minutes on a low shelf
in a moderate oven. (Generally parsnips are baked in
the same oven as the main meat dish, whose cooking
temperature governs that of the parsnips.)

BEACÁN BRUITHE (Baked Mushrooms) (pronounced *backon briha*)
    12-16 large field mushrooms
    4 oz. chopped onions
    4 oz. wholemeal breadcrumbs
    4 oz. sausagemeat
    2 oz. butter
    1 tsp. chopped sage
    salt and pepper

Wash and peel mushrooms. Remove stalks and
discard. Brush mushrooms with melted butter. Fry
onions in remaining butter. When tender, mix onion
and butter with breadcrumbs, sausagemeat, herbs
and seasonings. Divide among the mushrooms. Place

mushrooms in a shallow ovenproof dish, pour 4 tablespoons of water into bottom of dish and bake for 15-20 minutes in a moderate oven.

BRAISED CELERY

    1 head celery
    1 medium onion
    1 tsp. chopped parsley
    2 slices bacon
    $\frac{1}{2}$ pt. stock
    salt and pepper to taste
    1 oz. butter

Clean celery, cut into one-inch pieces and place in a casserole dish. Finely chop bacon and onion and sprinkle over celery along with chopped parsley. Pour on stock. Dot with knobs of butter. Cover dish and bake in a moderate oven for 30-45 minutes.

BRAISED ONIONS

    4 medium onions
    1 tsp. brown sugar
    1 tsp. chopped sage
    1-1$\frac{1}{2}$ pts. stock
    2 oz. butter
    salt and pepper

Peel onions. Place in a pot, cover with cold water and simmer for 15 minutes. Drain. Place in an ovenproof dish. Mix sage, sugar, stock, salt and pepper and pour over onions. Place a knob of butter on top of each onion and bake in a moderate oven for 2 hours.

BUTTER BEANS

$\frac{1}{2}$ lb. butter beans
$\frac{1}{4}$ lb. onions
2 oz. butter
salt and pepper

Soak beans overnight. Drain and place in a saucepan with enough cold water to cover. Bring to the boil and simmer for about 2 hours or until tender. (Do not season the beans whilst cooking as this will toughen the skins.) Fry the onion, finely chopped, in the butter until soft. Toss the cooked beans in butter and onions, season and serve.

DRESSED TURNIP

2 lbs. turnips
salt and pepper
bacon fat for frying

Peel turnips thickly to remove outer layers of skin. Chop into one-inch cubes. Cook in lightly salted boiling water until tender. Strain and roughly mash. Heat bacon fat in frying pan and gently fry turnip for 2-3 minutes.

Cold turnips may also be used, frying until heated through.

KEADY STEEPED PEAS

1 lb. dried peas
2 tsps. bicarbonate of soda (bread soda)
salt
4 rashers of bacon
$\frac{1}{2}$ lb. onions
1 oz. butter

Pour three times their volume of boiling water on peas; add a teaspoon of soda. Drain and place in pot with enough boiling salted water to cover. Bring to the boil and stir in a teaspoon of soda. Lower heat and simmer gently for 15 minutes. Chop onions and bacon rashers and fry slowly in butter until cooked. When peas are cooked, drain and place in serving dish. Spoon onions and bacon over them and pour on any butter left in pan.

NETTLES (as or with Cabbage)

'Twas down by the Glenside
I met an old woman,
A pluckin' young nettles,
Ne'er saw I was coming.

an Irish folk song

Nettles are said (and it is true) to be 'good for the blood'. Any Irish mother worth her salt would serve up a dish of young nettles to her family at least three times in the spring to purify their blood after the winter. Quite strong-tasting in themselves, a few cupfuls were often added to cabbage, so that the children didn't know they were eating them!

4 pints nettles or 1 medium cabbage
and 1 pint nettles
salted water or bacon water to cover

If using nettles only, bring water to the boil, add nettles and simmer for 10 minutes. If using cabbage and nettles, add cabbage to boiling water and cook for 5 minutes before adding nettles. Continue cooking for

10 minutes. Drain. (Reserve liquid for broth.) Add a knob of butter and serve.

TOMATOES IN BUTTER
   1 lb. fresh tomatoes
   $\frac{1}{4}$ lb. onions
   4 oz. butter
   salt and pepper

Finely chop onions and fry gently in butter until tender. Quarter tomatoes and add to pan. Cook gently until soft. Season and serve with bacon and fried bread. Do not use margarine or oil in this dish or cut down on the quantity of butter used, as this will destroy the flavour.

Bread

Along with the potato, the mainstay of the traditional Irish diet was bread — and indeed several types of bread are made with potato.

Yeast was never an ingredient in traditional bread-making. The raising-agents used were butter-milk and bicarbonate of soda, commonly known in Ireland as 'bread soda', or fresh milk, cream of tartar and bicarbonate of soda.

Nothing can beat the taste of a soda farl, hot from the griddle and dripping with country butter. Mind you, not everyone has the 'touch' for good bread-making, and the calibre of a wife was often judged by the lightness of the bread she baked.

APPLE BREAD

 1 quantity basic soda bread dough
 1 lb. stewed apples, sweetened to taste

Roll out half the dough to half an inch thick circle. Put cooked apple in the centre to within one inch of the edge. Moisten edges with milk. Roll out the remaining dough to the same size and place over the apple. Press edges well to seal. Cook gently on a griddle (or a heavy-based floured frying pan) until a light skin forms on top, then turn and cook for a further 10-15 minutes. Alternatively, bake in a moderate oven for 40-45 minutes.

CURRANT BREAD

 1 quantity basic soda bread
 6 oz. currants or any dried fruit

When lightly kneading the basic soda bread dough, incorporate the dried fruit and bake as for basic bread.

OATMEAL BREAD or OATCAKES

 6 oz. oatmeal
 2 oz. flour
 1 level tsp. salt
 $\frac{1}{2}$ pt. warm water

Mix flour and salt together. Slowly add warm water. Roll out on a floured board to $\frac{1}{4}$ inch thick. Cut into triangles. Cook on a pan or griddle until golden on both sides. Dry out in a cool oven (150°C, 300°F, Gas Mark 2) until crisp.

These cakes are eaten buttered, with a glass of

milk, for supper but are also good with oily fish such as herring or mackerel.

SCONES

1 lb. flour
2 oz. butter
1 level tsp. bicarbonate of soda
1 tsp. cream of tartar
$\frac{1}{2}$ tsp. salt
$\frac{1}{4}$ pt. buttermilk or sour milk
1 egg
milk or egg for glazing

Sift together flour, soda, cream of tartar and salt. Rub in the butter. Make a well in the centre and add egg and milk beaten together. Mix very lightly. Turn onto a floured board and gently roll to half an inch thickness. Cut into triangles 1-2 inches wide. Place on a floured baking tray. Glaze with milk or beaten egg and bake at 230°C, 450°F, Gas Mark 8 for 15 minutes.

Add 1 tablespoon sugar and 4 oz. dried fruit to mix after rubbing in the butter, for sweet scones.

SODA BREAD

12 oz. plain flour
$\frac{1}{2}$ tsp. salt
$\frac{1}{2}$ tsp. bread soda (bicarb.)
$\frac{1}{2}$ tsp cream of tartar
$\frac{1}{2}$ pt. buttermilk

Mix dry ingredients together and sieve twice — to incorporate plenty of air. Make a well in the centre of the flour and add enough buttermilk to get an easy-to-handle, soft but not wet dough. Knead very lightly, form into a round and mark with a cross. Bake in a hot oven 230°C, 450°F, Gas Mark 8 for 20 minutes. Reduce to 200°C, 400°F, Gas Mark 6, for a further 20 minutes.

The mark of the cross on the cake of bread is said to have been the Sign of the Cross and was to bring the blessing of Father, Son and Holy Spirit onto the bread so that none would be wasted.

This bread was made when butter was scarce, as it is complete in itself.

SODA FARLS
1 quantity basic soda bread

After kneading, roll dough to one inch thick round. Cut into four quarters. Cook each quarter (farl) on a griddle for 10 minutes on each side. Split and butter.

TEA BRACK
12 oz. flour
8 oz. sugar
12 oz. dried fruit
$\frac{1}{2}$ tsp. baking powder
1 tsp. mixed spice
1 egg
$\frac{1}{2}$ pt. hot tea

Soak the fruit overnight in tea. To the fruit and tea add lightly beaten egg and sugar. Sift together flour, spice and baking powder and add to fruit mix. Bake in a greased 7-8 inch square tin for $1\frac{1}{2}$ hours at 180°C, 350°F, Gas Mark 4. Cool in tin. Serve buttered.

Cakes

APPLE FRITTERS
Batter:
>   5 oz. flour
> $\frac{1}{4}$ pt. water
> $\frac{1}{4}$ tsp. salt
>   2 eggs – separated
>   1 tbsp. melted butter
>   2 large cooking apples
>   4 oz. sugar
>   lemon juice
>   oil for deep frying

Make batter at least an hour before required, using following method. Sift together flour and salt. Make a well in the centre. Add the cooled melted butter and some of the water and egg yolks. Work in the flour and beat until smooth. Add remaining water. Leave to stand. Just before using, beat the egg whites until stiff but not dry. Fold into batter mix. Peel, core and slice apples (slices about $\frac{1}{4}$-$\frac{1}{2}$ inch thick). Dip into batter and deep fry in very hot oil (175-180°C) until golden. Drain and serve dredged with sugar and sprinkled with lemon juice.

APPLE TART

1½ lbs. cooking apples
4-6 oz. sugar (to taste)
6 cloves
pinch nutmeg
12 oz. shortcrust pastry (made with 12 oz. flour,
    6 oz. butter)
egg yolk

Line a 9-inch greased pie tin with just over half the pastry. Peel the apples and slice thinly. Place in the pastry-lined tin and sprinkle with sugar, nutmeg and cloves. Roll out the remaining pastry, dampen edges and press onto pie tin. Fork around the edges and trim. Cut a cross in the centre of the pie. Cut four leaf shapes from pastry trimmings and stick around with water. Glaze with egg yolk — this gives a very shiny finish. Bake at 375°F, 190°C, Gas Mark 5 for 40 minutes or until golden.

BELFAST BOILED CAKE

1 lb. fruit
6 oz. candied peel
4 oz. glacé cherries
½ lb. butter
12 oz. sugar
12 oz. flour
1 tsp. baking powder
mixed spice
pinch salt

Put fruit in a saucepan. Cover with water and simmer gently for 5 minutes. Strain off water. Remove from

49

heat. Chop in butter, add sugar and mix well. Beat in eggs. Stir in all other ingredients. Pour into a 9-inch round, lined cake tin and bake at 350°F, 180°C, Gas Mark 4, for 1¾-3 hours. Check at 20 minute intervals after 1¾ hours. The 'wetness' of the boiled fruit is the cause of variation in cooking time.

CASTLECONNELL CAKE
   ¾ lb. flour
   6 oz. sugar
   3 eggs
   2 oz. butter
   2 oz. lard
   2 oz. candied peel
   ½ lb. currants
   ¼ lb. sultanas
   1 tsp. mixed spice
   1 tsp. baking powder
   ¼ pt. milk

Rub lard and butter into the flour. Sprinkle the baking powder over. Add other dry ingredients. Separate the eggs. Whisk the whites until stiff. Mix yolks with milk and add to dry ingredients. Fold in whites. Bake in a moderate oven 180°C, 350°F, Gas Mark 4, for one hour.

GINGERBREAD
   12 oz. flour
   4 oz. brown sugar
   8 tsps. treacle
   ¼ pt. milk

$\frac{1}{4}$ lb. lard
3 tsps. ground ginger
1 tsp. bicarbonate of soda
pinch of salt
1 egg

Sift together flour, salt, soda and ginger. Melt the lard gently and mix with treacle, sugar and milk. Beat egg and add to mixture. Gradually beat into the dry ingredients. Pour into a greased 6-7 inch square tin and bake for $1\frac{1}{4}$-$1\frac{1}{2}$ hours in a warm oven 160°C, 325°F, Gas Mark 3, until firm to the touch. Cool in tin and cut into squares.

PANCAKES

Irish pancakes are more like crumpets than today's usual *crêpes*.

1 lb. flour
3 oz. sugar
1 tsp. baking powder
$\frac{1}{2}$ tsp. salt
2 eggs
$\frac{3}{4}$ pt. buttermilk

Mix all dry ingredients together. Beat the eggs and add to the buttermilk. Mix well with dry ingredients. Cook on a hot greased griddle or pan. Pour in 3-inch cake tins. Turn when set on top and cook until golden. Butter when hot and sprinkle with sugar or syrup and lemon juice.

PORTER CAKE

1 lb. flour
½ lb. currants
½ lb. raisins
¼ lb. mixed peel
¾ lb. brown sugar
2 tsps. mixed spice
rind of 1 lemon
½ lb. butter
1 tsp. bicarbonate of soda
1 bottle of porter
4 eggs

Sieve the flour and rub in the butter. Add the fruit, spice, peel etc. Beat eggs. Heat porter and pour it over the soda. Pour porter and eggs over dry ingredients. Mix well and beat for 15 minutes. Bake in a well-greased tin in a moderate oven 180°C, 350°F, Gas Mark 4, for 2½-3 hours. Keep for a week before cutting.

SHORTBREAD

8 oz. flour
4 oz. cornflour
8 oz. butter
4 oz. castor sugar

Sift flour and cornflour. Add sugar. Rub in the butter. Knead until smooth and press into two greased 7-inch round tins, marking in triangles. Prick with a fork. Bake for 20 minutes in a moderate oven 180°C, 350°F, Gas Mark 4, then lower temperature to 160°C, 325°F, Gas Mark 3 (lower temp. if the shortbread begins to brown) for a further 20 minutes. Allow to cool in tins. When cool, cut along score marks. Sprinkle with castor sugar.

TIPSY CAKE

1 lb. stale cake (sponge, fruit etc)
2-3 tbsps. jam
1 measure whiskey
$\frac{1}{4}$ pt. sherry
$\frac{3}{4}$ pt. warm custard
$\frac{1}{2}$ pt. whipped cream

Break up the cake or cakes and gently mix through with jam – the mixture does not need to be completely even. Place in a glass bowl. Mix sherry and whiskey and sprinkle over cake. Press down lightly. Pour custard over the cake and chill. Spoon whipped cream over top and serve.

Drinks

BLACKBERRY CORDIAL

4 lb. blackberries
3 oz. sugar per pint of juice
$\frac{3}{4}$ pt. water

Soak berries in very lightly salted water for one hour. Rinse gently but thoroughly. Place berries in a saucepan with the water, bring to the boil, cover and simmer for an hour. Strain through muslin overnight. Measure the juice and add sugar at the rate of 4 oz. per pint. Bring to the boil and simmer for $\frac{1}{2}$ hour. Bottle and dilute as required.

CARRAGEEN

This is an excellent drink for a 'bad tummy'. Very easy to digest and highly nutritious.

$\frac{1}{2}$ oz. Carrageen moss
2 pts. milk
pinch of nutmeg and pepper
1 tbsp. sugar or honey

Soak Carrageen for 15 minutes in cold water. Wash thoroughly under running water. Place in a pot with the milk, sugar, nutmeg and pepper. Bring to the boil and simmer for 3 minutes. Strain and serve.

In place of the nutmeg other flavourings, such as ginger or lemon rind, may be used.

IRISH COFFEE

1 large measure Irish whiskey
2 tsps. brown sugar
strong hot coffee
lightly whipped cream

Heat 6 oz. stemmed glass. Half fill with very hot, strong coffee. (Place a teaspoon in the glass before adding the coffee to prevent cracking.) Add the sugar and stir until dissolved. Pour in whiskey and fill with coffee to within $\frac{1}{2}$ inch of the top of the glass. Spoon on lightly whipped cream and serve.

PUNCH

1 large measure Irish whiskey
1 tsp. sugar
$\frac{1}{2}$ slice of orange
$\frac{1}{2}$ slice of lemon
6-8 cloves

Stud orange and lemon slices with cloves. Heat tumbler, add sugar, orange and lemon. Stir in boiling water and whiskey. Serve on very cold days!

Miscellaneous

APPLE SAUCE
   1 lb. cooking apples
   2 tbsps. sugar
   knob of butter
Peel, core and chop the apples. Place in a pot with 2-3 tablespoons of water. Add sugar and simmer gently until the apple is cooked. Beat in the butter. Serve with pork and bacon dishes.

BUTTERMILK – HOMEMADE
   1 oz. yeast
   1 oz. sugar
   4 pts. water
   1 pt. milk
Cream sugar and yeast. Warm the water slightly and mix with milk. Gradually stir milk and water until the milk smells like buttermilk – slightly sour but not unpleasant. Strain through muslin and use for bread and scone recipes calling for buttermilk.

CARRAGEEN JELLY
   1 oz. Carrageen moss
   1 pt. milk
   2 dsps. sugar
   pinch of salt

Soak Carrageen for 15 minutes in cold water. Remove any roots or discoloured bits. Place in a saucepan with warmed milk and sugar and pinch of salt. Simmer (do not boil) for half an hour. Strain into a mould and leave to set. The addition of some stewed fruit pulp before allowing the Carrageen to set makes a very pleasant change.

DRISHEEN

4 pts. sheep's blood
2 pts. milk
2 cups breadcrumbs
$\frac{1}{4}$ tsp. thyme
$\frac{1}{4}$ tsp. allspice
salt and pepper
beef casings

Allow blood to set. Sprinkle with salt. Place in muslin and hang over a basin overnight. Discard muslin and residue. Stir the milk into the liquid in the basin. Add breadcrumbs and seasonings. Fill casings with mixture. Cook in boiling salted water for 5 minutes. Cool.

To serve, heat gently in a white sauce, seasoned with onions, or fry gently in butter for 2-3 minutes.

DULSE OR DILISK

Dulse, or dilisk, is a reddish-brown seaweed. It may be eaten raw in salads, as well as cooked in the following manner.

1½ lbs. dulse
8 oz. oatmeal
salted water for cooking
3-4 oz. bacon fat or butter

Soak dulse for 2-3 hours in cold water. Rinse well and remove all sand. Add to boiling salted water and simmer for 1-1½ hours until tender. Drain and sprinkle with oatmeal and fry in hot bacon fat or butter (the bacon fat is preferable) for 3 minutes each side.

FUDGE

1 lb. brown sugar
2 oz. butter
½ pt. cream

Place the sugar, butter and cream in a large, heavy-based pot. Heat until sugar and butter have melted. Bring to the boil and keep boiling until soft ball stage is reached. Remove from heat and beat until mixture is thick and beginning to harden. Pour into a well-greased tin and leave to cool. When almost set, cut into squares.

GOOGY

This peculiar-sounding dish is otherwise known as 'Egg-in-a-cup' and, believe it or not, seems to have a flavour entirely different to that of soft boiled eggs. It is a favourite with children and invalids.

1 soft-boiled egg
large knob of butter
salt and plenty or pepper

Take the top off the egg and carefully scoop out contents into a heated cup. Chop up roughly with a

knife, add butter, salt and pepper. Serve with bread
and butter.

LEMON ESSENCE

lemon peel
sugar

Soak large or small pieces of lemon peel in cold water
for 2 days. Drain and place peel in a wide-necked,
airtight jar and cover with sugar. The sugar will
eventually dissolve. (If the peel becomes uncovered,
add more sugar, or it will go mouldy.) Use one
tablespoon of the syrup to flavour cakes and puddings.

STIRABOUT

2 pts. water
4 oz. wheatenmeal or oatmeal
pinch of salt

If using oatmeal, soak the meal overnight in the water.
If using wheatenmeal, sprinkle meal into cold water
with a pinch of salt. Bring slowly to the boil, stirring
continuously. Lower heat and simmer for 10 minutes
for oatmeal and 20 minutes for wheatenmeal, stirring
occasionally. Serve with honey or top-of-the-milk.

YELLOW MAN

Did you treat your Mary-Ann
To dulse and yellow man
At the old Lammas Fair at Ballycastle-Oh?
  Irish folk song, 'Old Lammas Fair in Ballycastle-Oh'

6 tbsps. golden syrup
4 tbsps. sugar

1 tsp. sodium bicarbonate (bread soda)
1 tsp. lemon juice

Place syrup and sugar in a very large pot (liquid level will rise greatly whilst boiling). Boil, stirring constantly, until syrup forms hard, brittle threads when dropped into cold water (300°F). Stir in soda and lemon juice. Pour quickly into a well-greased, shallow baking tray. The 'Yellow Man' can now be left and broken into pieces when cold or, alternatively, when cool but still pliable, it can be removed from the tin and pulled, to give it a satiny finish, and cut into pieces.

Pulling: Pull the mixture into a sausage shape between the hands. Fold, twist and pull again. Repeat until it has acquired a shiny, silvery appearance. Shape into a length $\frac{1}{2}$-1 inch in diameter, cut into bite-sized pieces or small sticks and allow to cool.

ONION SAUCE
$\frac{3}{4}$ pt. milk
$\frac{1}{2}$ lb. onions, finely chopped
1 oz. butter
1 oz. flour
pinch of nutmeg

Gently fry the onions in the butter until soft (do not brown). Stir in the flour. Remove from heat and gradually add the milk, stirring constantly. Return to the heat and bring to the boil, cook for 2-3 minutes. Serve with lamb and bacon dishes.

RHUBARB AND GINGER PRESERVE

3 lbs. rhubarb diced
3½ lbs. sugar
rind and juice of 1 lemon
4 oz. crystallized ginger

Pour sugar over rhubarb and leave for one hour. Place in preserving pan with lemon juice and grated rind and bring slowly to the boil. Add crystallized ginger, cut into slivers. Boil rapidly for 10 minutes. Test for set — pour a little into a cold saucer; if the edges wrinkle slightly when tipped, the jam is ready. Pour into sterilized jars and seal.

RICE PUDDING

4 oz. pearl rice
2 pts. milk
1 oz. butter
4 tbsps. sugar
1 egg

Wash rice in cold water. Put into boiling water. Simmer for 10 minutes. Drain and place in dish. Add sugar, pour over beaten egg, milk, knob of butter and cinnamon. Cook gently in a low oven for 2 hours.

Folk Cures

BARLEY WATER
    3 tbsps. barley
    3 pts. water
    1 lemon
Wash barley in warm water. Put into pot with the water and sliced lemon. Simmer covered for 4 hours. It may be necessary to add more water during simmering. Strain and cool. One cupful before breakfast and ½ cup on going to bed was supposed to relieve weak kidneys.

BEEF TEA
    1 lb. leg beef
    2 pts. water
    salt to taste
Cut beef into cubes. Cover with cold water and leave overnight. Boil for 2 hours. Season. The meat is then discarded and the 'tea' given to invalids, convalescents or people suffering from anaemia.

BORAGE TEA
An infusion of borage leaves, sipped whilst hot, soothes and relieves chesty coughs.

COWSLIP TEA
    1-2 oz. cowslip blossoms
    1 pt. boiling water
Pour boiling water onto blossoms. Leave to infuse for 2 minutes. Strain and serve with a little honey if desired. This was used as a 'nerve tonic'.

DANDELION COFFEE

Wash and scrub thick dandelion roots. Dry in a warm oven until brown. Grind to a fine powder. Take $\frac{1}{2}$ to 1 teaspoon in boiling water with sugar to taste. One cup per day flushes the kidneys.

INDIGESTION CURE

$\frac{1}{2}$ pt. milk
pinch of nutmeg
pinch of pepper

Place milk, nutmeg and pepper in a small pot and bring to just under boiling point. A little sugar may be added for taste. Drink whilst still warm.

LEMON AND BLACKCURRANT DRINK

1 pt. water
1 lemon
2 tsps. blackcurrant jam

Cut up lemon and simmer in water for $\frac{1}{2}$ hour. Stir into blackcurrant jam for a comforting sore throat or cold remedy.

MUTTON FAT

To cure chapped hands, rub melted mutton fat into them every morning, after washing with warm water.

OATMEAL FACE PACK

1 egg
oatmeal to mix

Mix the egg with enough oatmeal to make a stiff paste. Pat into face and leave for 15 minutes. Rinse off with warm water.

This gently cleanses sensitive skin.

POMANDER
1 thin skinned orange
30 cloves
ground cinnamon

Stick the cloves all over the skin of the orange. Roll in ground cinnamon. Dry out in a very cool oven for 2 to 3 hours. Hang in a wardrobe or cupboard. This gives a refreshing scent to clothes.

ROSE HIP SYRUP
2 lbs. rose hips
sugar

Top and tail the hips. Cut in two and remove seeds and pith. Leave them in a covered dish until they are soft. Sieve them. Weigh the pulp and add an equal quantity of sugar, plus enough water to make a thick syrup. Bring to the boil and simmer for 10 minutes. Bottle. Take one to two teaspoons daily as a general tonic.

SORE THROAT REMEDY
Chewing a clove of garlic is said to relieve sore throats. Fresh parsley takes away the smell of garlic from the breath.

TREACLE
One teaspoon of treacle taken each morning in $\frac{1}{2}$ cup warm water was said to cure, or prevent, varicose veins.

UBH BÁN (pronounced *uv bawn*)

    2 egg whites

    $\frac{1}{2}$ tsp. castor sugar

Beat eggs until glossy. Add sugar. This was given to people with upset stomachs who could not manage solid food.